# Miles to Go

COLLECTED POEMS
BY ROBERT FROST

Illustrated by Evan Robertson

# Nature's first

# green is gold,

Her hardest hue to hold.
Her early leaf's a flower;
But only so an hour.

Then leaf subsides to leaf.
So Eden sank to grief,

So dawn goes down to day.

Nothing gold
can stay.

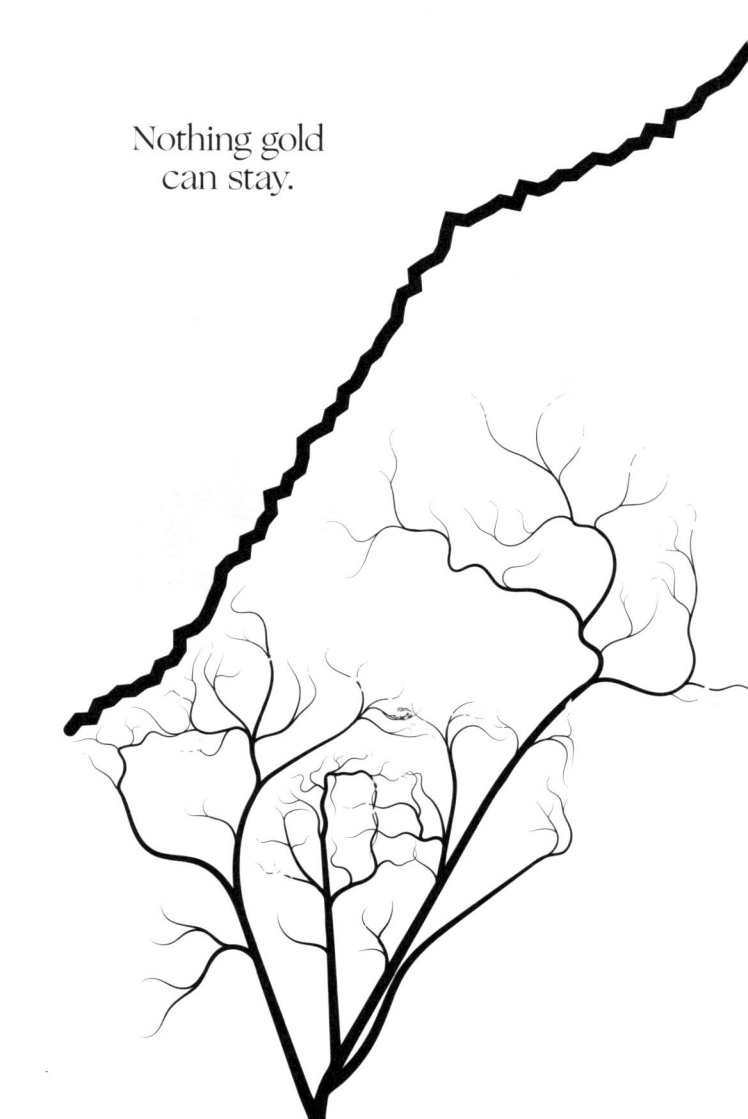

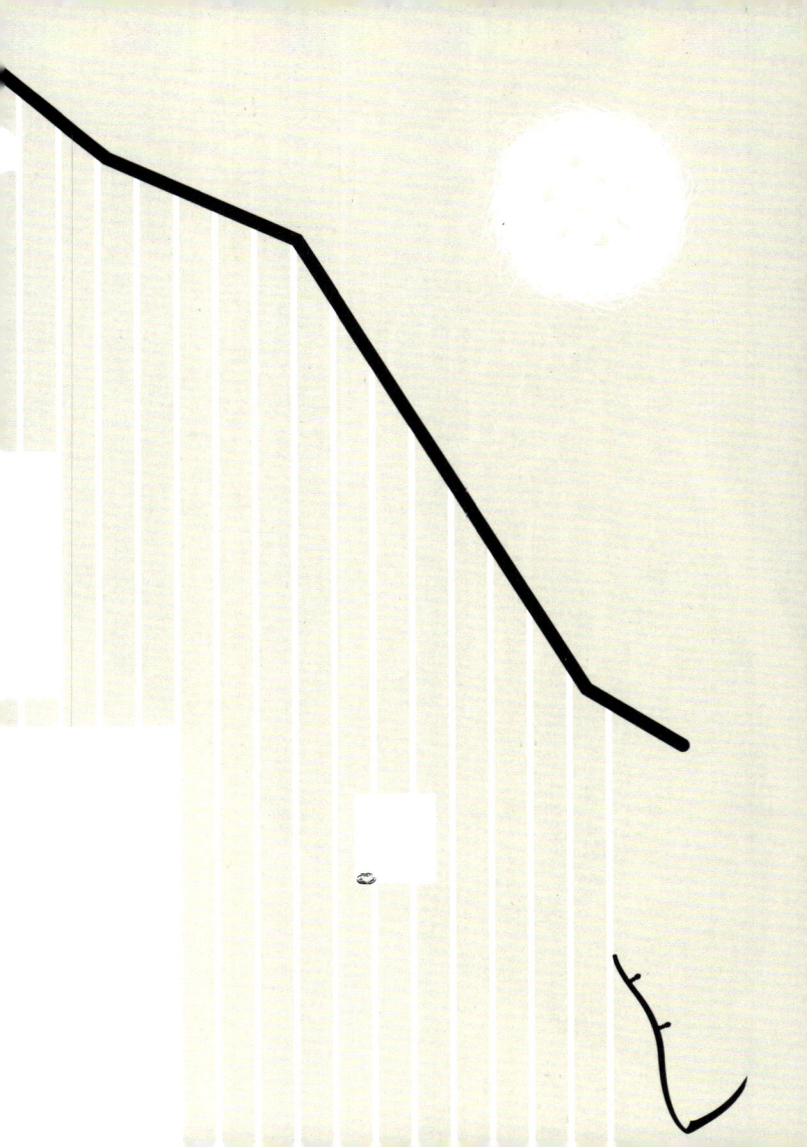

# There was never a sound beside the wood but one,

And that was my long scythe
whispering to the ground.

# What was it it whispered?
# I knew not well myself;

Perhaps it was something about the heat of the sun,
Something, perhaps, about the lack of sound—
And that was why it whispered and did not speak.

It was no dream of the gift of idle hours,
Or easy gold at the hand of fay or elf:

# Anything more than
## the truth
### would have seemed too weak

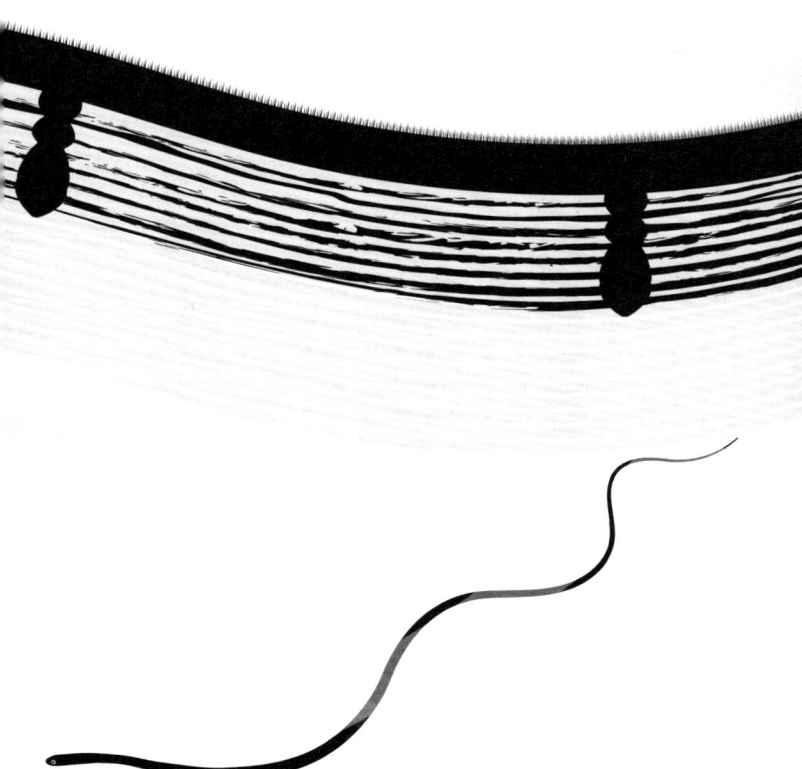

To the earnest love that laid
the swale in rows,

Not without feeble-pointed spikes of flowers
(Pale orchises), and scared a bright green snake.

# The fact
## is the sweetest dream that labor knows.

# Two roads diverged

# in a yellow wood,

And sorry I could not travel both
And be one traveler, long I stood
And looked down one as far as I could
To where it bent in the undergrowth;

Then took the other, as just as fair,
And having perhaps the better claim,
Because it was grassy and wanted wear;

Though as for that the passing there
Had worn them really about the same,
And both that morning equally lay
In leaves no step had trodden black.

I shall be telling this with a sigh
Somewhere ages and ages hence:
Two roads diverged in a wood, and I —
I took the one less traveled by,

There is
a singer
everyone
has heard,
Loud, a
mid-summer
and a
mid-wood
bird,

Who makes the solid tree trunks sound again.
He says that leaves are old and that for flowers
Mid-summer is to spring as one to ten.

He says the early petal-fall is past
When pear and cherry bloom went down in showers
On sunny days a moment overcast;
And comes that other fall we name the fall.
He says the highway dust is over all.

The bird would cease and be as other birds
But that he knows in singing not to sing.
The question that he frames in all but words
Is what to make of a diminished thing.

The house had gone to bring again
To the midnight sky a sunset glow.

> Now the chimney was all of the house that stood,
> Like a pistil after the petals go.

The barn opposed across the way,
That would have joined the house in flame
Had it been the will of the wind, was left
To bear forsaken the place's name.

No more it opened with all one end
For teams that came by the stony road
To drum on the floor with scurrying hoofs
And brush the mow with the summer load.

The birds that came to it through the air
At broken windows flew out and in,

# Their murmur
# more like
# the sigh
# we sigh

From too much dwelling on what has been.

Yet for them the lilac renewed its leaf,
And the aged elm, though touched with fire;

And the dry pump flung up an awkward arm;
And the fence post carried a strand of wire.

For them there was really nothing sad.

But though they rejoiced
  in the nest they kept,

One had to be versed
  in country things

Not to believe the phoebes wept.

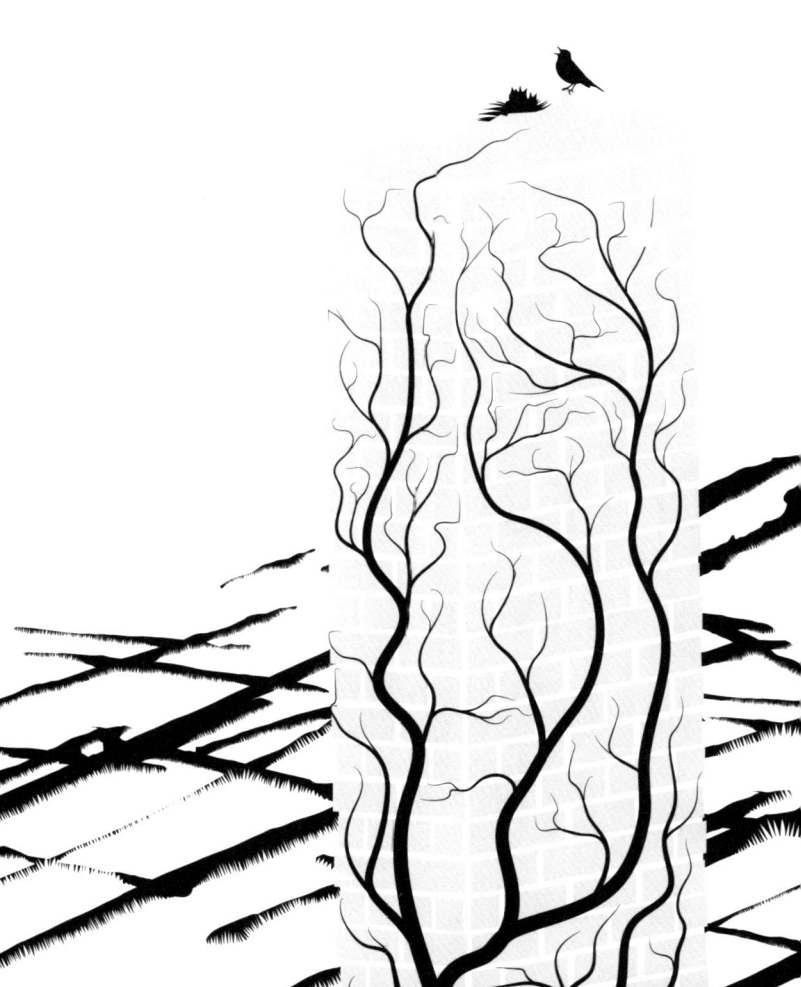

My long
two-pointed
ladder's
sticking
through
a tree
Toward
heaven
still,

*After Apple-Picking*

And there's a barrel that I didn't fill
Beside it, and there may be two or three
Apples I didn't pick upon some bough.

The scent of apples: I am drowsing off.
I cannot rub the strangeness from my sight
I got from looking through a pane of glass
I skimmed this morning from the drinking trough
And held against the world of hoary grass.

It melted, and I let it fall and break.

But I am done with apple-picking now.
Essence of winter sleep is on the night,

But I was well
Upon my way to sleep before it fell,
And I could tell

What form my dreaming
        was about to take.

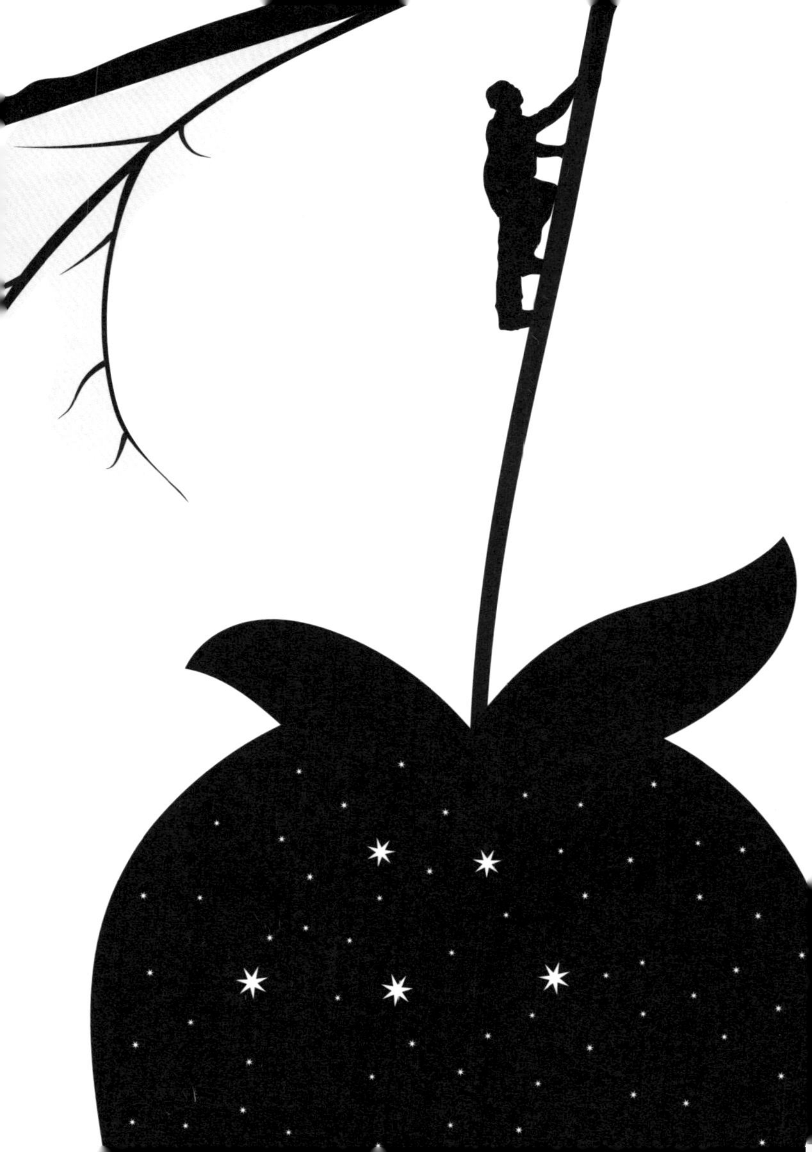

Magnified apples appear and disappear,
Stem end and blossom end,
And every fleck of russet showing clear.

My instep arch not only keeps the ache,
It keeps the pressure of a ladder-round.
I feel the ladder sway as the boughs bend.

And I keep hearing from the cellar bin
The rumbling sound
Of load on load of apples coming in.

For I have had too much
Of apple-picking:

# I am overtired

Of the great harvest I myself desired.

There were ten thousand thousand fruit to touch,
Cherish in hand, lift down, and not let fall.

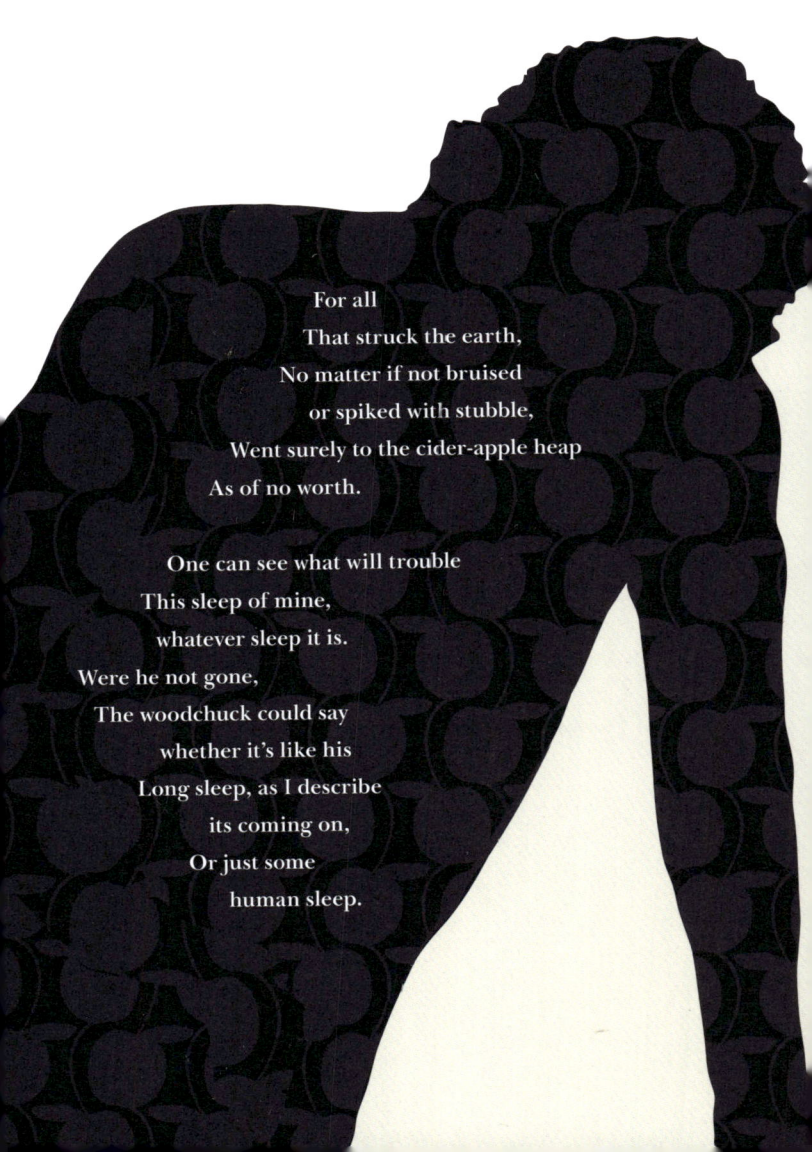

For all
That struck the earth,
No matter if not bruised
or spiked with stubble,
Went surely to the cider-apple heap
As of no worth.

One can see what will trouble
This sleep of mine,
whatever sleep it is.
Were he not gone,
The woodchuck could say
whether it's like his
Long sleep, as I describe
its coming on,
Or just some
human sleep.

# When
I see
birches
bend to left and right

Across the lines of straighter darker trees,
I like to think some boy's been swinging them.
But swinging doesn't bend them down to stay.
Ice-storms do that.
        Often you must have seen them
Loaded with ice a sunny winter morning
After a rain. They click upon themselves
As the breeze rises, and turn many-colored
As the stir cracks and crazes their enamel.

Soon the sun's warmth makes them
  shed crystal shells

Shattering and avalanching
  on the snow-crust--

Such heaps of broken glass
  to sweep away

You'd think the inner dome
  of heaven had fallen.

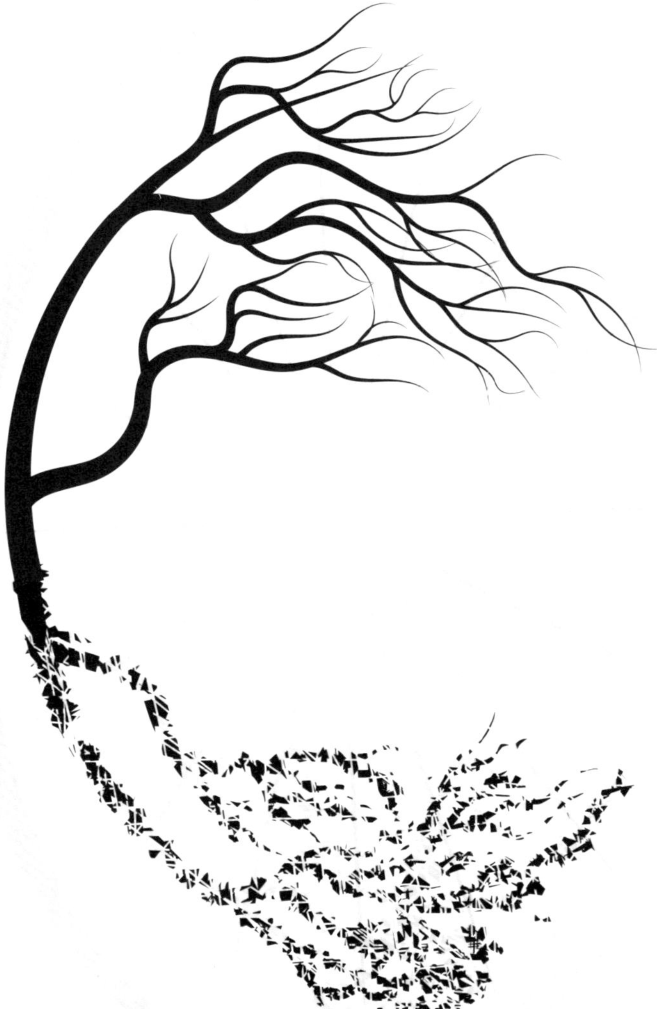

They are dragged to the withered bracken by the load,
And they seem not to break; though once they are bowed
So low for long, they never right themselves:
You may see their trunks arching in the woods
Years afterwards, trailing their leaves on the ground
Like girls on hands and knees that throw their hair
Before them over their heads to dry in the sun.

# But I was going to say

# when Truth broke in

With all her matter-of-fact about the ice-storm

# (Now am I free to be poetical?)

I should prefer to have some boy bend them
As he went out and in to fetch the cows—
Some boy too far from town to learn baseball,
Whose only play was what he found himself,
Summer or winter, and could play alone.

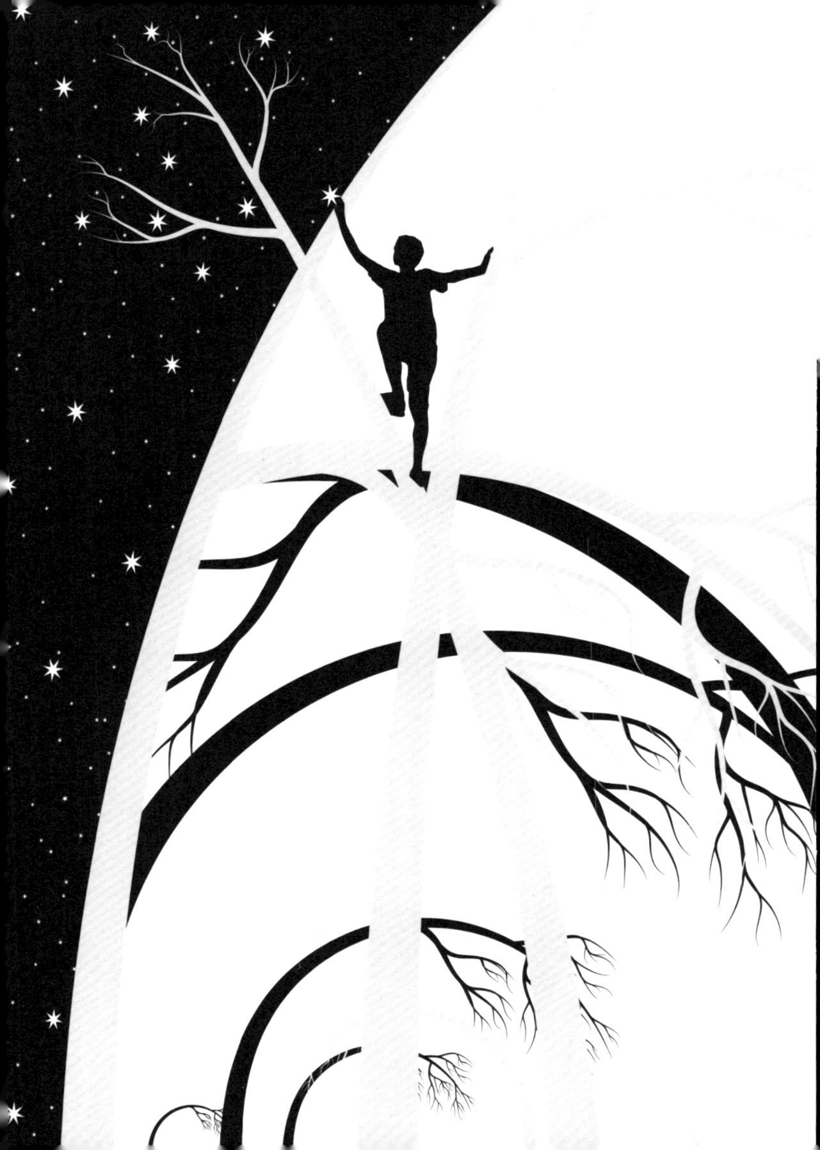

One by one he subdued his father's trees
By riding them down over and over again
Until he took the stiffness out of them,
And not one but hung limp, not one was left
For him to conquer.

                    He learned all there was
To learn about not launching out too soon
And so not carrying the tree away
Clear to the ground.

                    He always kept his poise
To the top branches, climbing carefully
With the same pains you use to fill a cup
Up to the brim, and even above the brim.

Then he flung outward, feet first, with a swish,
Kicking his way down through the air to the ground.
So was I once myself a swinger of birches.
And so I dream of going back to be.

It's when I'm weary of considerations,
And life is too much like a pathless wood
Where your face burns and tickles with the cobwebs
Broken across it, and one eye is weeping
From a twig's having lashed across it open.

I'd like to get away from earth awhile
And then come back to it and begin over.

May no fate willfully misunderstand me
And half grant what I wish and snatch me away
Not to return.

# Earth's the right place for love

I don't know where it's likely to go better.

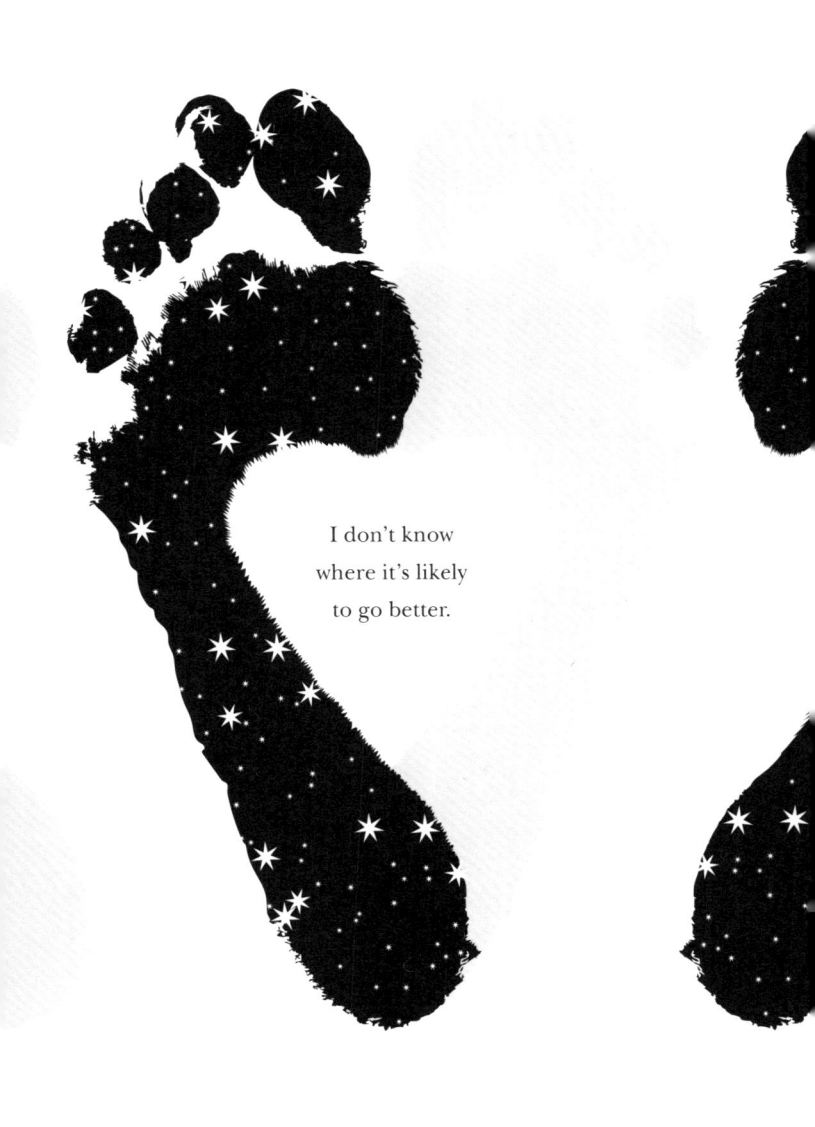

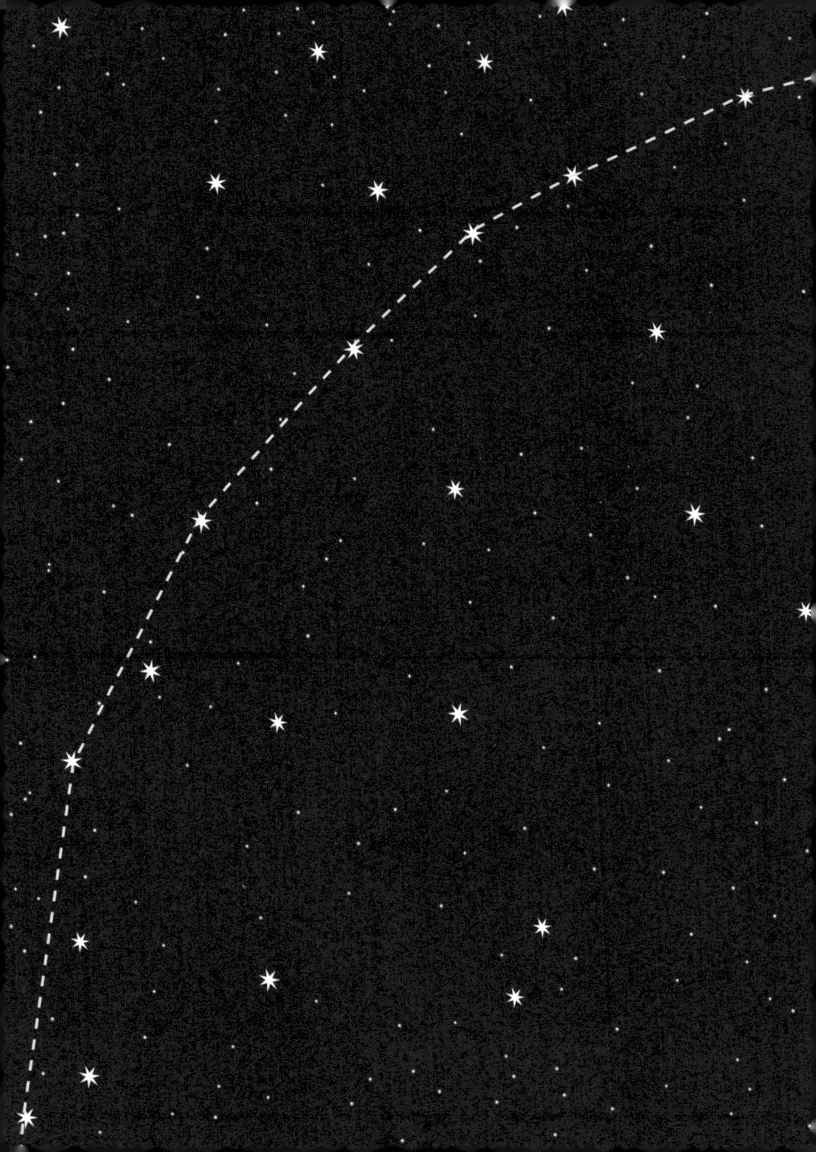

I'd like to go by climbing a birch tree,
And climb black branches up a snow-white trunk
*Toward* heaven, till the tree could bear no more,
But dipped its top and set me down again.
That would be good both going and coming back.

# One could do worse than be a swinger of birches.

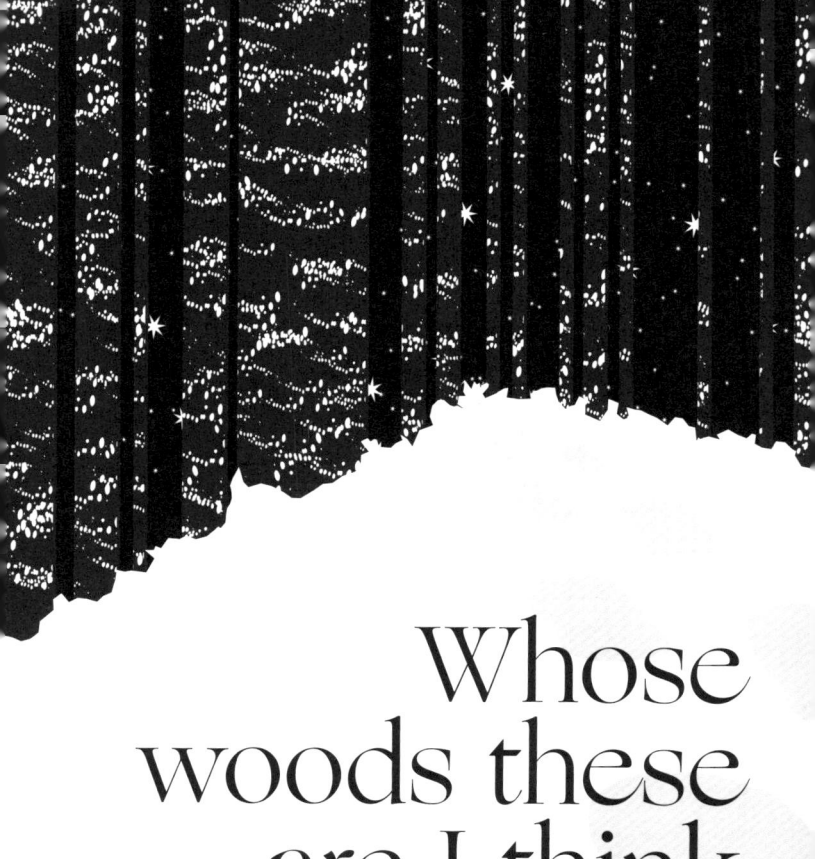

Whose woods these are I think I know

His house is in the village though;

He will not see me stopping here
To watch his woods fill up with snow.

My little horse must think it queer
To stop without a farmhouse near
Between the woods and frozen lake
The darkest evening of the year.

He gives his harness bells a shake
To ask if there is some mistake.
The only other sound's the sweep
Of easy wind and downy flake.

# The woods are lovely, dark and deep.

But I have promises to keep,
And miles to go before I sleep,

And miles to go before I sleep.

# He halted in the wind,

and—what was that
Far in the maples, pale, but not a ghost?

He stood there bringing March against his thought,
And yet too ready to believe the most.

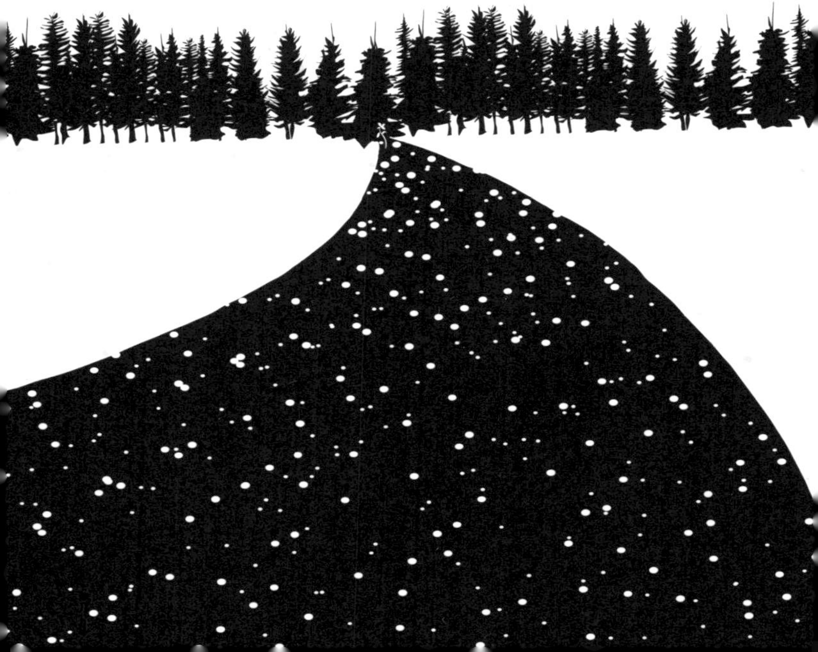

"Oh, that's the Paradise-in-bloom," I said;
And truly it was fair enough for flowers

Had we but in us to assume in march
Such white luxuriance of May for ours.

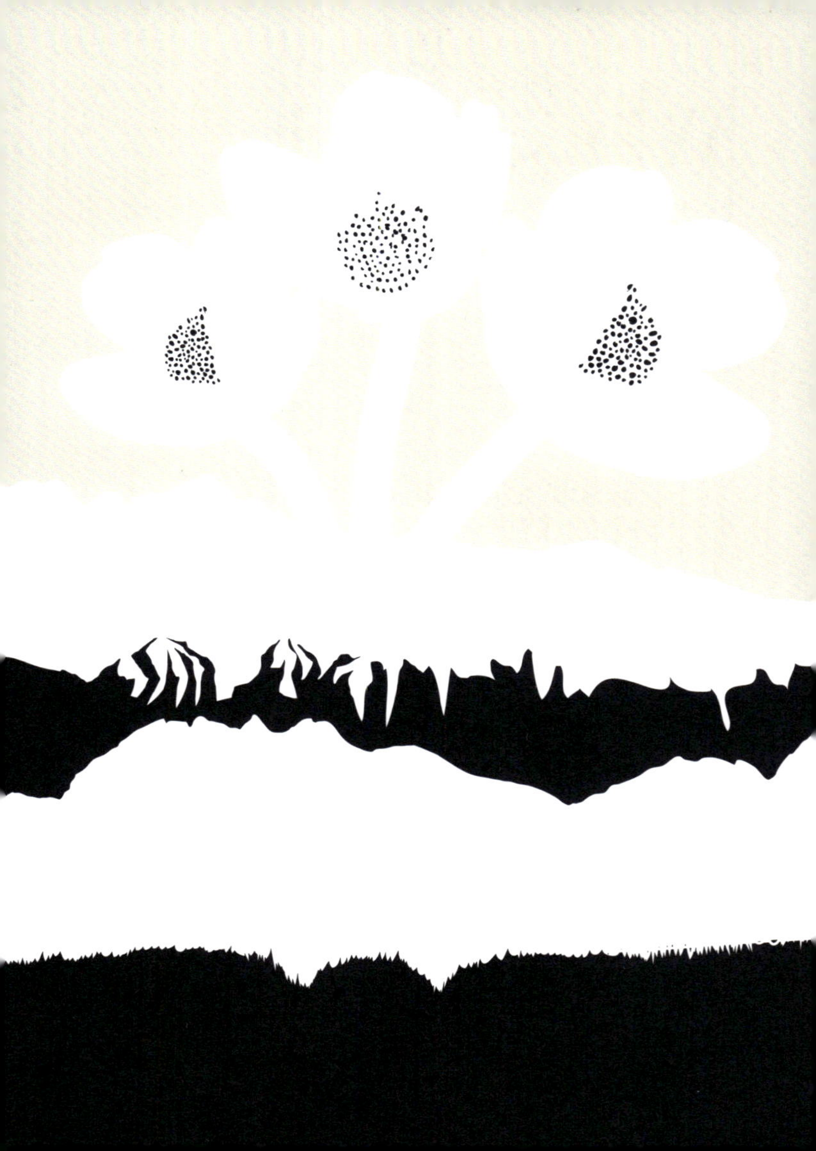

# We stood a moment so

Myself as one his own
pretense deceives;

And then I said the truth
(and we moved on).

# in a strange world,

A young beech clinging to its last year's leaves.